Famous Cows of the Bible
Six Studies for Personal Devotion or Small Groups

Brant D. Baker

*To Community Presbyterian Church of Cambria
who have generously shared
caring, contentment, and the occasional cow*

Cover: Original watercolor by Kathi Rippe

Copyright 2018 by Brant D. Baker
ISBN-13: 978-1722916664
ISBN-10: 1722916664

Table of Contents

Introduction
~7~

Seven Fat Cows
Genesis 41:1-4
~9~

The Cattle on a Thousand Hills
Psalm 50:1-15
~15~

The Calf and the Bear
Isaiah 11:1-9
~23~

The Cattle Are Lowing
Luke 2:1-20
~29~

The Fattened Calf
1 Samuel 6:1-16, 2 Samuel 6:1-16, Matthew 22:1-10
~35~

Golden Cows
Exodus 32:1-6
~41~

Introduction

A number of years ago, reluctantly, but with my wife's steady prodding, I wrote an adult small group study called *Famous Donkeys of the Bible.* Imagine my surprise (and my wife's exultation) as that has proven to be one of my most popular studies! More recently, God brought us to the central coast of California, a rural region midway between Santa Barbara and San Francisco. Here are vast ranches, numerous wineries, and large stands of oak and pine. There are one hundred year old barns, a comfortable pace of life, and cows, lots and lots of cows.

So naturally, that got me to thinking about the famous cows of the Bible. Turns out there are quite a few, but they are, we might say, hidden by our vocabulary. The word "ox" is much more common in biblical usage, and unless you had a very particular upbringing you might not know that an ox is simply a male cow trained for the work. Beyond these sturdy plodders there are a number of more well-known cows, including those featured in Pharaoh's dream, the calf that "miraculously" appeared out of Aaron's fire, and the faithful ox-like creature in the throne room of heaven.

View of Santa Lucia Mountains, Cambria, CA – author photo

The following six studies can be used in small groups or individually. In used in a small group each participant can have a copy, but in any case a leader should read the sections aloud.

One of the things cows do is to chew their cud, which is the marvelous system God has provided for them to find nutrition in what otherwise is a very poor source of nourishment. For us chewing the cud is an apt analogy of the approach we are to take toward scripture, slowly processing it, revisiting it, patiently seeking all that God has to offer from what is otherwise a very *rich* source of nourishment. May we be fed as we do so!

Seven Fat Cows

DISCUSS/REFLECT
Are you a person who plans ahead or who lives more spontaneously?

READ
Genesis 41:1-4

DISCUSS/REFLECT
What questions does this passage raise for you?

READ
God gave Pharaoh a dream that got his attention, and behind the dream—actually a pair of dreams—is a lesson about planning ahead. Actually God gave Pharaoh a pair of dreams, with a pair of strong symbols. The second dream featured "stalks of grain," which represented a staple food source, but this study isn't about famous grains of the Bible, so we'll set that aside.

God gave Pharaoh a dream, a dream that carried a powerful message, and then, because God is good, God gave Pharaoh a way to understand it! As it happened, the interpreter was languishing in prison, and here a brief review is needed (you can find the full story in Genesis 37, 39-45).

Joseph, as you may remember, was the favorite son of his father, his youngest, to whom he gave the famous coat of many colors. This favoritism did nothing to endear Jacob to his siblings, but things got worse, as he showed an early propensity to interpret dreams, and a youthful propensity to annoy his older brothers. Joseph told his brothers of dreams in which they bowed down to him, and they took their revenge by selling him into slavery and passing him off as dead to their father (as with many biblical families, these guys put the "fun" in dysfunctional!).

Once in Egypt Joseph ends up as a servant in the home of a high-ranking official named Potiphar. Joseph does well in this new post, and is given a high level of trust by his new master, but there is a problem. We learn in Genesis 39:6 that Joseph was "well-built and handsome," and he catches the eye of Potiphar's wife. He resists her, but she doesn't handle rejection well, and makes a false report against him. Joseph lands in jail, but the Lord was with him, and showed him kindness and favor (Genesis 39:21).

Sometime later two of Pharaoh's servants also get put in prison – the chief cup bearer and the chief baker—and Joseph is assigned to take care of them. (We don't know their crimes, perhaps the one served merlot with the fish, and the other made the chocolate chip cookies a bit too crispy.) They each have dreams, which Joseph is able to interpret with God's help. The chief baker is killed (just as his dream predicted), and the chief cup bearer is restored, but despite Joseph's pleading to have the man bring his case to Pharaoh, the chief cup bearer forgets about the whole messy incident.

Forgotten, that is, until God's perfect time. Two years later is when God gives Pharaoh the dream that gets his attention. None of Pharaoh's magicians and wise men can discern it's meaning, however, which suddenly reminds the chief cupbearer of his shortcomings. "'Pharaoh was once angry with his servants," he confesses," and he imprisoned me and the chief baker in the house of the captain of the guard. Each of us had a dream the same night, and each dream had a meaning of its own. Now a young Hebrew was there with us, a servant of the captain of the guard. We told him our dreams, and he interpreted them for us, giving each man the interpretation of his dream. And things turned out exactly as he interpreted them to us: I was restored to my position, and the other man was impaled.'

"So Pharaoh sent for Joseph, and he was quickly brought from the dungeon. When he had shaved and changed his clothes, he came before Pharaoh. Pharaoh said to Joseph, 'I had a dream, and no one can interpret it. But I have heard it said of you that when you hear a dream you can interpret it.' 'I cannot do it,' Joseph replied to Pharaoh, 'but God will give Pharaoh the answer he desires.' (Genesis 41:10-16).

The rest, as they say, is history. God gives Joseph the interpretation, and on the strength of this interview, Joseph goes on to become the second most powerful man in the empire. In that role, of course, he is later able to take care of his family in the midst of the famine, and of course, his brothers do end up bowing down before him.

DISCUSS/REFLECT
Why do you think God allows unresolved injustice or unjustified pain?

Reflect on a situation when you or others had to wait for resolution or redemption.

Do you think God wants us to lament? Why or why not?

What brings you peace in the midst of experiencing or witnessing unjust suffering?

Have you ever had a dream you felt predicted or foreshadowed a future event? Was it disturbing or comforting? Did any aspect of your dream come to pass?

READ
My friend Bob is a cattle rancher. He and his family live on land that has been passed down going on ten generations. He has roots, and he knows cows.

Cattle have been raised on the central coast of California since the late 1700's, brought by the missions, which raised cattle for the hides. Following a severe drought the area flirted with dairy cows from the late 1860s until the 1950s, but dairy cows take a lot of year-round grass to keep up production.

Bob would say that the life cycle of beef cattle is short and sweet. Generally calves are born in the fall, when the hills are just starting to turn green with the winter rains. Within a month or two a calf will start munching away, and will grow from a birth weight of around 70 pounds to about 750 pounds in about nine months. A full grown Angus cow will tip the scales at 1200 pounds, while a bull will weigh in at closer to 2000 pounds. By the way, it seems that the roughly 1.5 billion cattle populating the world today came from a small herd of now-extinct bovines called aurochs. Aurochs were found across the entire Eurasian continent (including northern Africa), and were the cattle and oxen of biblical Palestine and Egypt (knowledgenuts.com).

God gives Pharaoh two dreams, and the first features seven cattle, sleek and fat. You can almost see Pharaoh licking his lips as he sleeps thinking about all those steaks! They graze among the reeds, but then the scene changes. As Pharaoh later explains to Joseph, "After them, seven other cows came up—scrawny and very ugly and lean. I had never seen such ugly cows in all the land of Egypt. The lean, ugly cows ate up the seven fat cows that came up first. But even after they ate them, no one could tell that they had done so; they looked just as ugly as before. Then I woke up" (Genesis 41:19-21).

Pharaoh's pride of livestock is noted—we couldn't possibly have such ugly cows in Egypt! But there may be more than county fair bragging rights in Pharaoh's comment: it turns out that several of the Egyptian deities are depicted in bovine form, including Hathor, Apis, Montu (as Bakha), and Ra (through the cult of the Mnevis bull). This last may be the most significant as Ra was believed to have created all forms of life, and the Egyptians sometimes called themselves "the Cattle of Ra" (wikipedia.org/wiki/Ra).

Mnevis bull 12th century BCE, from Heliopolis - Photo: Rufus46 - CC BY-SA 3.0

In other words, God is making a spiritual statement in choosing to deliver the message to Pharaoh about what is coming. "Your gods may look handsome today," God seems to be saying, "but tomorrow is another day, and your gods won't be up to the challenge. The abundance you assume comes from them will not be remembered..." Yahweh is giving a compassionate word of warning and preparation, and showing further compassion by saying it in Pharaoh's language. The whole thing is quite moo-ving.

All around us we see people putting faith in false gods, gods that look good today, but which will fail when the ugly times come. Just to name a few, our culture values physical appearance, material wealth, and science. This despite the fact that beauty fades, wealth dissipates, and science changes its mind about what is "true" almost every day. As Christians our response needs to reflect the compassion of our God, as we gently and urgently communicate that only Jesus Christ is the same yesterday, today, and forever (Hebrews 13:8).

DISCUSS/REFLECT
What are some of the sleek cows in today's culture? What are some of the sleek cows that you see changing? Are they changing in good or bad ways?

What are some of the false gods in which people put their confidence, but which are likely to fail when crisis comes? In what ways does God supply warning about the shortcomings of these false gods? How can Christians speak lovingly to those around us who have put their faith in these false gods?

READ
These seven fat cows make for a terrific story of betrayal, heart break, restoration, and celebration. And through it all we see the mighty hand of God at work, reaching back across the years to redeem the evil intended by Joseph's brothers to take care of them, then redeeming the evil intended by Potiphar's wife to put Joseph on a path to meet Pharaoh, and even redeeming the forgetfulness of the chief cup bearer, all in preparation for the time when Joseph's gift would have the greatest impact.

There are several take-aways here, the first being that there is wisdom in planning ahead. This advice isn't unique to the Bible, but it surely can be found there, in such guidance as to consider (you sluggard) the ways of the ant. It has no commander, no overseer or ruler, yet it stores its provisions in summer and gathers its food at harvest (Proverbs 6:6-8). Plan ahead, be disciplined, and good things can happen!

More substantively, the promise of God to be our rock, our fortress our deliverer, our refuge, our shield, our salvation, and our stronghold (Psalm 18:2) is a promise we can rely on. It may take ten or fifteen years, perhaps even longer, but God is always faithful. Always. When we find ourselves in a pit, in prison, falsely accused, betrayed, forgotten by supposed friends, still God is with us, unfolding His purpose for our lives. God will not be confused or defeated by our enemies. God has a plan and our task is to wait patiently for it. With confidence we can hold to the promise that God's revelation will be revealed at the appointed time; "it speaks of the end and will not prove false. Though it linger, wait for it; it will certainly come and will not delay (Habakkuk 2:3).

These are aspirational goals. God knows our frame. In our better moments we carry these truths in our head and heart. In more normal times we find them afresh in daily reading God's word. In stressful times we surrender to the strength of the community of faith around us, who uphold us in prayer, compassion, and love.

Our role, it seems, is to know that what someone intends for evil, God uses for good. Ours is to put our hope in God, for we will yet praise him. We are to be still and know. We are to hold fast to the conviction that all things work together for good for those who love God. We are not to lose heart, but believe and ask God to help our unbelief. We are to not grow weary in doing good, to be content whatever the circumstances. Our is to run the race, to rejoice always, to press on. All this we can do, through Christ Jesus who strengthens us!

DISCUSS

How does the story of Joseph give us hope?
What are some practical ways you have found to help you not lose heart, not grow weary in well doing, and to be content in whatever circumstance?

PRAYER

Pray together as a group in your usual manner.

The Cattle on a Thousand Hills

DISCUSS/REFLECT
Describe an encounter you have had with nature in which you realized just how small you were, and how great is our God.

READ
Psalm 50:1-15

DISCUSS/REFLECT
What questions does this passage raise for you?

READ
Hopefully you have had the experience of knowing just how small you are. It's healthy to realize that despite our pretensions, we are transitory, finite, and tiny. Maybe it was on a camping trip, asleep under a sky vast with stars; maybe it came out on the ocean, looking out over the horizon that never ends; maybe standing on the edge of a mighty water fall, watching millions of gallons of water rush over the cliff and fall in thunder; perhaps it came as you climbed a mountain which you earlier saw from a great distance away on the valley floor, but now as you labor up its great girth and height, everything is suddenly put in perspective.

Grand Canyon North Rim – author photo

I've had many of these experiences, but somehow nothing speaks to me of my smallness like the Grand Canyon. Like millions of tourists I've stood on the rim and looked out, and then looked down, and been dizzied by the scope and scale of it all. Some years ago, my son and I hiked the Canyon rim to rim. The maps say it is about twenty four miles, but maps are flat and don't account for going a bit more than a mile down (from the North Rim), and then almost another mile back up again (to the South Rim). We hiked it in one long day and it remains one of the greatest tests of physical endurance I've ever undertaking. But besides the joy of accomplishment, and the great bonding time with my son, it gave me an even greater insight into how insignificant we are as we scurry back and forth across the face of this small planet.

Nature can be humbling if we let it, which is why the Psalmist uses the vastness of nature to talk of the even greater vastness of the Almighty God. "The Mighty One, the Lord, speaks and summons the earth from the rising of the sun to where it sets...a fire devours before him, and around him a tempest rages. He summons the heavens above, and the earth, that he may judge his people (Psalm 50:1-4).

Pastor Louie Giglio has put together some great video presentations on the size of the heavens above, what scientists can only call "the known universe," because truth be told, they don't rightly know how big it is. The "measuring stick" astronomers use is called a light year, the distance light can travel in a year, which is 5.88 trillion miles. You and I live in a little galaxy called the Milky Way, which is 100,000 light years across, or 100,000 times 5.88 trillion miles. To put this in perspective, our solar system—the collection of planets of which Earth is one, circling the sun—our solar system is about the size of a quarter, and the Milky Way Galaxy is the size of the entire North American Continent in relative size. In other words, we aren't really more than a blip inside the Milky Way, and on that scale, the Grand Canyon is barely a wrinkle.

Giglio continues by noting that our sun is one of the billions of stars the Milky Way. If you counted one per second, he notes, it would take you 2,500 years to count them all. But our galaxy is among hundreds of billions of galaxies in the *known* universe. Our nearest spiral galaxy neighbor is Andromeda, which is two and a half million light years away. In 2016 the Hubble Space Telescope calculated the distance to the most far-out galaxy ever measured, which has the catchy name of GN-z11. It is so far away that the light reaching the earth from it is over 13 billion years old (Louie Giglio, "Indescribable," youtube.com).

When you try to wrap your mind around things like the billions of stars in our galaxy and the hundreds of billions of galaxies in the known universe, it can be pretty disorienting, but that's probably a good thing. Giglio calls it "significant insignificance," because while we are small compared to the scale of the universe, we are still important to our loving God. God knows who we are, and what's more, God knows *what* we are, and still God loves us through Jesus Christ.

DISCUSS/REFLECT

What is the biggest number with which you have had personal experience? Perhaps it was the distance you flew on a trip to another country, perhaps it was the size of the check you had to write for the down payment on your house, or perhaps it was the number of seconds you had to wait for an important event in your life. Share your personal experience of a big number with the group.

What is your reaction to Giglio's idea of "significant insignificance?" How does this idea either help or hinder your view of yourself and your view of God? Given our insignificance in the universe, how then do you react to the fact that God loves us?

READ

Still, it seems we can't resist trying to make ourselves even more significant to God, and usually God isn't impressed. In Psalm 50 God tells the people that, while he has nothing against their sacrifices *per se,* the fact is that God has no need of their bull...or their goats. Why? Because "every animal of the forest is mine, and the cattle on a thousand hills. I know every bird in the mountains, and the insects in the fields are mine" (10-11). (I know this study is about famous cows of the Bible, but you have to like God claiming ownership of "the insects of the fields...!")

I grew up in a Baptist church in El Cajon, California. I have fond memories of singing "He Owns the Cattle on a Thousand Hills," written by John Peterson.

> He owns the cattle on a thousand hills
> The wealth in ev'ry mine
> He owns the rivers and the rocks and rills
> The sun and stars that shine
> Wonderful riches more than tongue can tell
> He is my Father so they're mine as well
> He owns the cattle on a thousand hills
> and I know He cares for me!

The point of this happy children's song is first, that God is all-sufficient, and second, that there is nothing we can do or say that will make God love us any more than God already loves us in Jesus Christ. That's why God says through the Psalmist, "If I were hungry I would not tell you, for the world is mine, and all that is in it. Do I eat the flesh of bulls or drink the blood of goats? 'Sacrifice thank offerings to God, fulfill your vows to the Most High, and call on me in the day of trouble; I will deliver you, and you will honor me" (Psalm 50:12-15).

DISCUSS/REFLECT

In what ways to people try to impress God with service or offerings?

As Christians we understand that to obey is better than sacrifice. But it is also true that obedience is a form of sacrifice. How do you see "sacrifice as obedience" being played out in your life or in the lives of those around you?

What would "a sacrifice of thank offerings to God" look like in your life?

READ

The direction of Psalm 50 is similar to that of Micah 6:6-8. "With what shall I come before the LORD," asks the prophet, "and bow down before the exalted God?" He then attempts to answer his own question. "Shall I come before him with burnt offerings, with calves a year old?" Micah starts smallish, wondering if a calf will do it, but then quickly escalates, "Will the LORD be pleased with thousands of rams, with ten thousand rivers of olive oil?" Then, to show how such thinking can get out of hand, Micah even offers the dark prospect of child sacrifice, "Shall I offer my firstborn for my transgression, the fruit of my body for the sin of my soul?" The clear answer to all of this, and especially the last, is "NO!" Instead God now speaks through the prophet to give the answer God prefers, "He has shown you, O mortal, what is good. And what does the LORD require of you? To act justly and to love mercy and to walk humbly with your God."

To do justice is to have compassion for and take care of those who are weak and vulnerable in our midst. In the days of Amos that meant widows and orphans, and so in our day too, but also in our day, to do justice on behalf of the teenager who comes from a broken home, who has an undiagnosed mental condition, who begins to self-medicate using illegal drugs, or who seeks comfort in sexually risky behaviors. In our day doing justice also means taking care of the woman who was perhaps once that same teenager and now finds herself living on the streets, a victim of her own choices no doubt, but also a victim of many other forces beyond her control. In our day to do justice could also have something to do with the needs of the illegal alien who doesn't know anything about the politics of immigration, only that his wife and baby back home in Sonora are hungry and there is a place of perceived opportunity to the north—He has told you, O mortal, to do justice...

DISCUSS/REFLECT

What is your "serving passion" before God? To whom or to what do you feel called to serve as an offering to God?

Who in your life right now could benefit from you doing justice to their cause?

What are your God-given gifts for service? Do you believe you are making full use of those gifts?

What should someone do who doesn't have a passion in their heart right now?

READ

And to love kindness. The word "kindness" is *chesed* in Hebrew. The same word shows up in Hosea, when God says, "I desire steadfast love—*chesed*—and not sacrifice, the knowledge of God, rather than burnt offerings" (Hosea 6:6). In Micah's prophecy we get a third meaning for *chesed* that rounds out its meaning even further: kindness. We could also use mercy or pity. It all goes to how we treat those around us.

In the commencement address delivered to my graduating class from seminary author Frederick Buechner told us to first, be kind; to second, be kind; and third, to be kind.

Be kind to those who are closest to you, those we tend sometimes to treat the worst. Do not neglect the everyday kindnesses of saying "please" and "thank you" even to the spouse with whom you have shared a home for thirty years or more. Treat your children with kindness, granting them the common dignity and respect due to all people, that they may thrive in your home. Be kind to those closest to you.

Then, be kind to those you work with. Not because it is always deserved, but if only to invite them to step into a kinder world then the one they perhaps inhabit. Be willing to set aside the cut throat office politics, the trite office gossip, the petty office insults and slights. Be kind to those you work with.

And finally, be kind to everyone you meet. Our society teeters on the brink of a major breakdown every day, as the social capital that helps bind us together is eroded by countless insults, slights, and slanders, on the one hand, and countless missed opportunities to express gratitude, to compliment, in short, to be kind. Being kind in all our encounters means seeking opportunities to upbuild another human being in whatever exchange we are in: from store clerks to waitresses, yes, even from bureaucrats to telemarketers. He has told you, O mortal, to be kind to *everyone* you meet.

DISCUSS/REFLECT

As Christians we are kind because God has poured kindness into our lives. What is it in your life that speaks most to your heart about God's kindness to you?

Who in your life could use an act of kindness this week?

How do you express kindness when you aren't feeling it in return or in kind?

READ

And finally, our God says that we are to walk humbly with him. Please note that God doesn't ask that we walk in perfection. God asks simply that we walk in humble recognition of our reliance on the one who made the heavens and all the stars that fill them. God asks that we remain ever aware of our need to receive from the One who owns the cattle on a thousand hills. And, God asks that we humbly submit ourselves to the grace-filled relationship offered to us in Jesus Christ, not trying to save ourselves, calling on him in our troubles for deliverance. He has told you, O mortal, to walk humbly with your God.

PRAYER

Pray together as a group in your usual manner.

ON YOUR OWN

Reflect on how God in Christ has saved you in this past week, and/or on a situation in your week ahead in which you will benefit from walking with Christ in mindful humility.

The Calf and the Bear

DISCUSS/REFLECT
What is your favorite "wild" animal and why?

READ
Isaiah 11:1-9

DISCUSS/REFLECT
What questions does this passage raise for you?

READ
A man once visited a zoo and as he went from cage to cage came at last to a sight he could hardly believe. There in the same cage was a cow lying down with a bear. The cow didn't seem afraid, the bear didn't seem hungry, both of them seemed quite happy to be together. . Over the cage was a sign that said, "The Peaceable Kingdom." The man went home and told his family, who didn't believe him, but agreed to come and see with their own eyes. The went, and sure enough, there was the cow, there was the bear, both of them in the same cage without any apparent problem.

As they took in the scene the zookeeper happened to come by. "This is fantastic," exclaimed the man. "How on earth do you manage this?" The zookeeper smiled and said, "It's quite easy, really, we put in a new cow every morning..."

The prophecy found in Isaiah 11 falls nicely into three parts, including the very famous vision of the peaceable kingdom, which we will get to shortly, but before we do, look at this reconstruction of the temple menorah (next page). A temple menorah is related to, but not exactly the same as, the nine-branched menorah used on Hanukah, and which commemorates the miracle that a day's worth of oil lasted eight days. The seven-branched temple menorah is one of the oldest symbols of the Jewish faith, and is understood by many Jews to be a reminder of Israel's mission to be "a light unto the nations" as described in Isaiah 42:6. But the origins of this lampstand go back to instructions found in Exodus 37, which command that a lampstand of pure gold be made, with six branches going out, three on either side. These branches were to be end in cups shaped like almond blossoms, which is intriguing because of a later story found in Numbers 17, when the staff of Aaron sprouted and put forth buds, then blossoms, and finally ripe almonds, as a special sign of God's favor.

As you may know, seven is one of the holiest numbers in the Bible. There are seven days in creation, and there are also seven words in the Hebrew translation of Genesis 1:1.

The Temple Institute, Jerusalem - Public Domain

In English the verse says, "In the beginning God created the heaven and the earth." In Hebrew, reading from right to left, it says ב.ר.א.ש.ית, ב.ר.א א.ל'ה.ים, א.ת ה.ש.מ.י.ם, ו.א.ת ה.א.ר.ץ which transliterates to "Barasheet bara Elohim et ha'shamayim v'et ha'retz." The fourth word, which is to say, the word in the middle of the seven, is א.ת, "or "et" in transliteration. Jewish scholars call "et" the untranslatable word. Its function is to indicate that a direct object of the sentence is next. "Et" is formed from the letters *aleph* and *tav*, the first and the last letters of the Hebrew alphabet. In Greek, those letters would be alpha and omega, and as such we could imagine that "et" might be the Genesis version of the more familiar statement of Jesus found in Revelation, "I am the Alpha and the Omega." It's as though, in the center of these profound words of creation, God planted a symbolic reminder of Christ being the first and the last in all things.

So, getting back to the menorah, and back to Isaiah 11, we first have a description of God's Messiah in terms reminiscent of

Aaron's rod, in this case a shoot coming out from the stump of Jesse, which is to say that out of the complete destruction Israel will face at the hands of the Assyrians, out of the bare stump that will remain, God will bring forth a shoot, a branch that we might even call the True Vine. And from this shoot will sprout what Jewish piety calls the six gifts of the Spirit: wisdom, understanding, counsel, might, knowledge, and fear of the Lord.

Maybe we could call this a description of a menoric messiah! Whatever the case, this image of a tall lampstand with six additional lamps is indeed a fitting description of God's promised king, one who, Isaiah goes on to tell us in the second part of this text (verses 3-5), will judge with righteousness, deciding with fairness and equity in favor of the meek, those who have been persecuted and subjected, while at the same time striking down the wicked with only a word.

In its original context this would have been a comforting word of promise, even as the oak of Israel was about to become the stump of Jesse at the hands of the Assyrians, who were on their way at this point in history. God is promising a coming king to the nation who, unlike the kings before him, will not abuse his power, but instead use it for good. "He will not judge by what he sees with his eyes, or decide by what he hears with his ears; but with righteousness he will judge the needy, with justice he will give decisions for the poor of the earth. He will strike the earth with the rod (there's that word again) of his mouth; with the breath of his lips he will slay the wicked. Righteousness will be his belt and faithfulness the sash around his waist."

These are words that comfort us just as they comforted Israel. Many are the times in our lives we are falsely accused, played for the fool, taken advantage of, or maliciously attacked. In language reminiscent of many psalms, we know we can rest in a Messiah who is righteous judge, who will vindicate, who will bring righteousness, who is our stronghold and deliverer.

DISCUSS/REFLECT

What is the significance do you attach to finding the word "et" in the middle of the Genesis 1:1?

Are there situations in your life right now that need God's faithful judgment and righteous deliverance? Share as you are comfortable...

What does the passage from Isaiah say about injustices we see around us? What promise is offered, what hope is given?

READ

The promises of Isaiah 11:3-5 move to the third part of the text, which in a sense seems to move beyond the contemporary setting to an anticipated future. Certainly we would have to agree that Isaiah's vision of the peaceable kingdom remains unfulfilled, and yet strangely compelling, since God has given us the ability to hope.

The vision of the lion and the lamb, the cow and the bear, fascinates us, since we understand that only in Jesus Christ can such a hope will be realized. Many of us have probably sent or received Christmas cards featuring paintings by the 18th century artist Edwards Hicks. Hicks, who was also as a Quaker minister, and is thought to have painted as many as one hundred versions of this scene. Why so many? Dale Rosenberger, a Congregational minister in Ridgefield Connecticut suggests that study of the evolution of these paintings shows the carnivores become more and more ferocious and the herbivores more and more vulnerable. As Hicks paints throughout his life the miracle of peace seems even more far-fetched.

How well we know it. We have only to read the newspaper or watch the evening news to hear stories of cows being put into the bear's cage, as adults abuse children, as men exploit women, as the rich mistreat the poor, as whites oppress persons of color.

Of course we need not look at the newspapers to know all this, we can simply look in the mirror. In Jekyll and Hyde fashion we know that at some point or another we all grow fangs and claws. It may be simply a momentary thing--the way we react to the shopper who seems oblivious the long line that everyone else is standing in. Or it may be that the carnivore aspect of our nature is more long term--a manner of living life that tends to oppress and dominate.

But the truth, the divine truth that penetrates to our core and unmasks all our pretensions, this truth is that we are all wolfs, and lions, and bears sooner or later, more or less. We all have that dark, vicious side of ourselves, a side that calculates and schemes and looks for vulnerabilities in those around us. Perhaps part of Isaiah's prophetic vision, and part of God's promise to us, is the hope that our inner carnivore can be finally put into its proper place, it's power and might harnessed for the purpose God intended, whatever that might be.

DISCUSS/REFLECT

In what venue of your life (work, family, recreation) do you see the greatest departures in yourself from who you most aspire to be? In what arena do you struggle most with your inner wolf, lion, and bear?

How does the Christian doctrine of sin help describe and manage what we see in ourselves and what we see around us?

READ

There may be little we can do to change the terrible and horrifying zoo that we all live in, a world in which we often find ourselves to be the new lamb of the day being lowered into the lion's den. That world will have to wait with groaning for its full redemption until Christ's final coming, in which he will fulfill all that God intends for his menoric messiah.

There is, however, an antidote for our Jekyll and Hyde sickness, a cure for the unbridled carnivore that lurks in each of us. It is that we welcome Jesus Christ into our own interior zoo, asking him to shine his menorah into the dark corners of our lives, showing us those parts of ourselves that need to be changed. What hidden pride influences the ways we interact with others? What secret shame mutates even our best intentions? What buried wound twists steals our joy? Only the one who was there at creation and who will be there at its completion has the power to tame all of the creatures that lurk within each of us.

In her children's book, *Dance in the Desert*, Madeleine L'Engle tells of a young couple who long ago traveled through the desert with their child. They traveled with a caravan on their way to Egypt and had to pass through a desert filled with ferocious beasts. Some people were afraid of the beasts, and especially afraid that they might harm the child in their midst. One night, as they were all sitting around the fire, a great lion appeared at the edge of the camp and everyone trembled. But the child held out his arms, and the lion rose up on his hind legs and of all things, began to dance. Then from the desert came running animals of all sorts: mice and donkeys, eagles and a snake, an ostrich, a pelican, and even two dragons and a unicorn. And they all bowed to the child and they all danced together round and round him as he stood at the center and laughed with delight.

You know this child's name. He is master of the zoo we call our world, and he will bring about a peaceable kingdom in our midst. For this we rejoice!

DISCUSS/REFLECT

What steps can we take to change our attitude when we find ourselves becoming jaded about this weary world of ours? How does being part of a community (the church) help us hold on to the promise of God's peaceable kingdom?

PRAYER

Pray together as a group in your usual manner.

The Cattle Are Lowing

DISCUSS/REFLECT

What is your favorite Christmas carol? Are there special memories attached to this?

READ

Luke 2:1-20

DISCUSS/REFLECT

What questions does this passage raise for you?

READ

The cattle are lowing, the baby awakes, but little Lord Jesus, no crying he makes.
I love thee, Lord Jesus! look down from the sky, and stay by my cradle till morning is nigh.

So says, and sings, the second verse of one of the most popular Christmas carols of all time, "Away in a Manger." But there are a couple of difficulties, starting with the supposed authorship of this beloved favorite. A great number of older hymnals title the carol as "Luther's Cradle Song."

But Richard Hill, in a study done in 1945, suggests that *"Away in a Manger"* might have originated as part of a play about Luther celebrating Christmas with his children, perhaps in connection with the reformer's 400th birthday in 1883 (wikipedia.org/wiki/Away_in_a_Manger).

Setting aside this difficulty, brings us to a different challenge: Luke tells us that there were shepherds living out in the fields, "keeping watch over their flocks by night." The use of the word "flock" tells us that these shepherds were keeping sheep or goats. The distinction between flock and herd is common usage, and can be very easily seen in Leviticus 1:1-13 having to do with different types of burnt offerings. "If the offering is a burnt offering from the herd, you are to offer a male without defect....You are to slaughter the young bull before the LORD... If the offering is a burnt offering from the flock, from either the sheep or the goats, you are to offer a male without defect (Leviticus 1:1, 5, 10).

Had Luke used the word "herd" we would surmise that the shepherds were keeping cattle. But that is not what Luke says, and actually, we shouldn't be surprised. There is no evidence that in biblical times cows were kept for their milk. In 1 Samuel 6:7-8 we hear of a milch cow (that is, a cow kept for her milk or giving milk), who is put to work drawing a wagon. But as the pastureland for grazing milk cows was much more scarce in Palestine than for goats, the likelihood is that the milch cow was in milk to feed a calf. As an aside, it is also likely that any cheese made in biblical times was primarily made of milk from goats (and possibly camels) (International Dictionary of the Bible, Vol 1, p 724)

We are led to the conclusion that any famous manger cows with the baby Jesus were most likely oxen, which is to say, male cattle who had been deprived of reproductive privilege. Oxen were the "work horses" of the ancient world, used for hauling and plowing, generally with some degree of training in order to acclimate to the yoke involved in these tasks. As it says in Proverbs 14:4, "Where there are no oxen, the manger is empty, but from the strength of an ox come abundant harvests."

So, no cute little Jersey milk cows here looking down on the baby Jesus. Descended from the ancient auroch, any oxen at the manger weighed in at a ton, stood nearly six or seven feet at the shoulder, and sported fierce horns as much as 30 inches long!

Our imaginations tend to recoil at such a picture, which may be the most useful aspect of this story concerning famous cows of the Bible: they put us in touch with the gritty realism of our Lord's birthplace. Forget about cute little Linus standing on stage at the Christmas pageant, reciting these lines from Luke, and think for a moment about what it must have really been like. J. Barrie Shepherd tells of a family vacation to Vermont. "After church," he says, "we drove out to the family farm for lunch. Later we went round to the sheds for milking time. The smell was almost enough, and the footing, but we were finally driven out by the flies that landed everywhere in vast, buzzing, swarming clouds." He continues, "Strange, but I've never seen a

Christmas card with flies buzzing in Joseph's ear; or with the mire, the noise, the pests, and the stench that are a basic part of an honest to goodness, honest to Godness, cowshed somewhere in the hills of Palestine" (*Faces at the Manger*, J. Barrie Shepherd, pp. 27-28).

The stark reality of the animals points our attention to the people. To begin, a couple of poor Jewish teenagers, traveling a long way, giving birth without benefit of family or friends or even a decent room. And then, showing up later, the shepherds. We've painted such sweet pictures of them in the manger around the baby Jesus that we've lost sight of just how earthy and, in fact, crude, these men were. Think about it: get past the Christmas card renderings and the Christmas carol sentiments and imagine with me what a shepherd was really like. Let's face it, a shepherd was not out there because he was well educated, rich, powerful, or well-mannered. These were men who lived with sheep all day, every day, who had dirty fingernails and smelled bad.

DISCUSS/REFLECT

Why might it be important that the birth place of Jesus had hulking oxen, buzzing flies, and a stench of manure and mire?

Does this more stark portrayal of the manger trouble you, confuse you, comfort you, or create some other emotional response? Explain.

READ

In his book, *Windows on Christmas,* Bill Crowder notes that David had been a shepherd on these very hillsides, guarding the flocks of his father. In later times this area was the primary supplier of sheep to the temple at Jerusalem. In the first century, he notes, there may have been more than 250,000 sheep offered annually at the Passover festival, a preponderance coming from Bethlehem (Bill Crowder, *Windows on Christmas,* 52). But these shepherds would never have seen the fruit of their labor. "Their work, among other things, required their hands-on participation in the birthing of lambs (which would bring them into contact with blood) and disposing of dead lambs (which would bring them into contact with dead bodies)—both of which made them ceremonially unclean... It seems so sad that the very individuals who were responsible for raising sacrificial lambs for the temple in Jerusalem were themselves excluded from the temple because they were considered ceremonially unclean" (53).

These filthy, faithful shepherds were going about their work with a kind of plodding goodness, night after night carrying out their duty, until on this night something happened. God came near and they became the first to hear of the amazing thing God was up to. It's as if God is going out of His way to make Jesus as lowly and humble as possible. And, it's as if God wanted to reassure us all that the inbreaking grace and joy and hope of Jesus Christ is available to all, because if God is well pleased to come near to a shepherd, then it seems very likely that God would be pleased to come near to us as well.

Of course, most of us tend not to think so. Oh sure, Zechariah was a priest, and Mary was obviously special to God. But what about you and me? Who are we that God should come near to us? The answer is that we're just the kind of folks God loves—earthy, crude, vulgar, plodding, with dirty fingernails and body odor and bad breath. As astounding as that sounds... God is well pleased to be with you, yes even the likes of you.

DISCUSS/REFLECT

How do you think the invitation by the angels to the shepherds changed them? Why do you think God might have invited them first? What might be the significance in the manger being, in many ways, the complete opposite of the Temple in Jerusalem?

It seems unlikely that God only prefers people with dirty fingernails. Instead, what are the character traits represented by the shepherds we might want to imitate?

Why do we tend to think that God is not please to come near us?

READ

Father Gregory Boyle has spent a lifetime working among the gangs of Los Angeles and in 1992 launched Homeboy Bakery, an ambitious project meant to give unskilled ex-felons what they need most, a job. In his book *Tattoos on the Heart* Father Greg talks a lot about the self-image of the gang members he works with, or more properly said, their lack of self-image. On occasion, he will do an intake on a homie who comes into their office looking for one of their services: tattoo removal, job placement, counseling, etc. "If I had a dollar for every time the following happens," he says, "I could close down my development office. I have the intake form, and I'm interviewing the homie seated in front of me.

"How old are you?"

And the homie says, "Me?"

And I'm thinking, No, what's your dog's age? We are the only ones in the room, and he says, "Me?" "Well, yes, you." "Oh, I'm eighteen."

"Do you have a driver's license?" "Me?" (Again, I think, No, I was wondering if your grandmother is still driving.) "Yes, you."

"No, I don't have a license."

The toxicity of self-hatred, says Boyle, gets so internalized that it obliterates the "me." The gang member can't believe that anyone would possibly have interest in knowing things about him…sure you're not talking about somebody else— who happens not to be in the room? (Gregory Boyle, Tattoos on the Heart, 51-52, Simon & Schuster, Inc.. Kindle Edition, 2010)

The deep mystery of the manger is that over and against our damaged self image, opposite our strong conviction that we are dirty, unworthy, sinners—which we are—is the miraculous truth that it is exactly people like us who God breaks in upon with a pronouncement of Good News…that no matter what we have done, no matter who we have been, no matter what our failures, Christ is for us. And if Christ be for us, who can be against us?

Luke says that Mary laid Jesus in a manger. As most Christians know, the word translates as "crib" but means the kind of crib you put fodder in to feed an animal. As such it was covered with the drool of ox, sheep, camel, and donkey. It probably had bite marks and rough, split wood. God's promised Messiah, the fulfillment of the eternal plan of salvation, the king of the Universe, comes not with fanfare, but with humility, and all in all, it's not really a pretty picture.

Dennis Swanberg tells the story of a Christmas pageant in which the innkeeper was a "special" young boy. Born with Downs' Syndrome, Robert was never able to do everything his brothers and sisters could do, but he did what he could.

One year he was asked to play the role of the Innkeeper in the Christmas pageant. His line was kept simple, "No room in the inn." He practiced day after day, and when the big night came, Robert was ready.

Things were going along nicely and when Mary and Joseph arrived and asked for a room, Robert was ready with his line. "No room in the inn." But rather than turning and going right away, Mary started to ad lib, "Please, can't you make any space for us?" Then Joseph got in on the act, "Yeah, can't you give us a room?" They had no way of knowing the effect this had on Robert, whose heart wanted one thing, but who knew his line. With a big tear rolling down his cheek he bravely repeated, "No room in the inn."

Realizing they had strayed outside the script, Mary and Joseph turned to leave. Before they got offstage, however, inspiration struck and Robert, bounding after them said, "Wait, you can have my room!" ("Swan's Place," December 20, 1997)

Will you give away your room, that room in your heart, to Jesus?

DISCUSS/REFLECT
What might be preventing you from making space for Jesus in the messy manger of your heart?

PRAYER
Pray together as a group in your usual manner.

The Fattened Calf – Sacrifices and Celebrations

DISCUSS/REFLECT
Besides holidays (like Easter, Thanksgiving and Christmas) and birthday cakes, are there special foods your family turns to for celebrations? Or, are there foods that you associate with times of grief, sorrow, or even guilt?

READ
1 Samuel 6:1-16

DISCUSS/REFLECT
What questions does this passage raise for you?

READ
My wife knows that for my birthday each year I will make the same request: a select grade steak for me to grill, an onion (also to be grilled), barbeque beans, and a nice bottle of red wine. Nothing says celebration for me like a T-bone on the barbeque!

Longtime rancher Bob Soto, whose people helped settle the central coast of California, remembers his uncle, in a heavy Italian accent, saying "Kids, don't fall in love with the cows." Seems like good advice: given the demands we have for both celebration, and in Old Testament times, for sacrifice, the life of a cow is bound to be short.

There are a pair of stories in the writings of the prophet Samuel that show how cattle were used for celebration in Old Testament times. In 1 Samuel 6:3-16 the Ark of the Covenant is being returned by the Philistines, who haven't enjoyed their time holding it captive. They have suffered terribly from the wrath of God, and so they load the Ark on a new cart hitched to a pair of cows that have calved but have never been yoked. The point of using both a new cart and "new" or untrained cows is to show reverence (compare Jesus riding a donkey on which no one had previously ridden). The point of the cows having recently calved and now separated from their calves is meant to see if this whole business is truly of the Hebrew God. If the cows leave their calves it would be taken as a sign of divine action (*The Pulpit Commentary*, 2010, BibleSoft, Inc.). (This, by-the-way, is the only mention of milk cows, "milch cows," in the Bible, and in this instance is simply because the cows have recently calved. As noted in the previous study, there simply isn't enough grass in the Holy Land to sustain dairy cows).

The end is not good for these two cows. When the cart came to the field of Joshua of Beth Shemesh in Israelite territory it stopped, whereupon the people there chopped the wood of the cart and sacrificed the cows as a burnt offer to God (1 Samuel 6:14). This is a thank offering as we find from time to time in the Old Testament (see, for example, Leviticus 7:15, 22:29, Psalm 107:21-22). And what could be a more appropriate end for cows that, at this point, have been set aside for holy service to God.

DISCUSS/REFLECT

Have you ever offered something to God in thanksgiving? Perhaps you received a gift, or a bonus at work, and made some sacrifice in connection with it.

If this hasn't been your experience, can you imagine what might be the circumstances that would bring about such an offering on your part at some future time? If you were to make such a thank offering to God, what would you likely offer?

READ

2 Samuel 6:1-16

DISCUSS/REFLECT

What questions does this passage raise for you?

READ

The second story of sacrifice surrounding the Ark of the Covenant comes in 2 Samuel, when it was finally time to move the Ark from its temporary home to Jerusalem. The move does not go well. David first brings 30,000 men, an obvious show of military force, and God is not impressed. They have barely begun when the oxen pulling the cart get distracted by the grain of a threshing floor, and Uzzah, one of the men guiding the procession reaches out to steady the Ark as the oxen stumble. He is struck down by God for his "irreverent act, and he dies (2 Samuel 6:6-7).

Uzzah is an innocent victim. He was simply trying to save the Ark from crashing on the ground. In larger perspective it may be that he was the focus of God's anger against David for the wrong-headed nature of the whole spectacle. Whatever the case, David tries again some months later, this time with less military fanfare and more faith-filled rejoicing. And, relative to our theme, when those carrying the ark had taken six steps, David sacrificed a bull and a fattened calf.

Some have supposed that David did this *every* six steps, which at a trip of close to twenty miles, would have been a lot of beef. More likely is that the sacrifice happened once those carrying the Ark had gone farther than the previous conveyance, and thus assured of God's approval, David made his sacrifice and danced before the Lord with all his might (2 Samuel 6:13-15).

The more fitting attitude David brings to this second move attempt is one of pure and thankful joy, so much so that he dances before the Lord with all his might. I once knew a pastor who would go to a hilltop near her home to dance in exactly this same way. I thought it was a beautiful picture, a worshipper alone before her God, dancing in joy and thankfulness, making an offering of self, pure and without pretense.

This seems to be the difference between the two attempts at moving the Ark. In the first, David wants to be seen, watched, noticed by others. In the second he doesn't care what anyone thinks. As he later says to Michal, daughter of Saul, who despises David for his display, "I will celebrate before the LORD. I will become even more undignified than this, and I will be humiliated in my own eyes (2 Samuel 6:21-22).

DISCUSS/REFLECT

Personally speaking, what might be your most pure and unpretentious way of worshipping God? Some people dance, some sing (alone) before the Lord, some write poetry or paint, not for public display, but only for God's glory and pleasure. What is your sacrifice of praise?

READ
Matthew 22:1-10

DISCUSS/REFLECT
What questions does this passage raise for you?

READ
Besides their use as sacrifices, many of the famous cows of the Bible are noteworthy for their nourishment. Specifically, they are part of a celebratory banquet, or at least in the parables of Jesus, as when the prodigal returns, or when there is a wedding.

The parable of the wedding feast found in Matthew 22 (and similarly in Luke 14:16-24) features "oxen and fattened cattle" prepared as part of a large banquet. Jesus tells this parable to the chief priests and the Pharisees, and it is the third is a series with similar themes (the Parable of the Two Sons and the Parable of the Tenets found in Matthew 21:28-46), all of them with essentially the same message: that the ones who were first favored and included have turned their back on God, therefore others will be invited in their place.

As is often the case with the parables of Jesus, it helps to use our spiritual imaginations and really see the scene he paints with words. And so imagine those formal banquet tables, beautifully appointed for the feast, now surrounded by strangers good and bad, poor and crippled, blind and lame. Now instead of people who understood proper decorum, the wedding hall was filled with guests who "oooed" and "ahhhed" over the incredible feast they were about to enjoy. One has to smile over the merry clatter these hungry replacement guests would make. Free of the muzzle of propriety they might have dug in with both hands, literally, until the servants rushed in to instruct them on proper decorum. And, as the well-aged wines flowed, they would likely become even more animated, with hoots and hollers to one another. "What do you think of us now, Stachys?" one of them might have cried to a friend. "I think that just yesterday we were lords of the dung, but today we are lords of tongue," his mate might reply. "Very clever, Stachys, and now pass me some of the calf's tongue that my own might taste twice!" (Brant Baker, *The Rest of the Story, Vol 1*).

DISCUSS/REFLECT

What's the most sumptuous meal you've ever enjoyed? What was the occasion and what foods were part of the celebration? Or, if you were going to plan the ultimate celebration feast, what would you be sure to include on the menu?

READ

Even if oxen and fatted cows aren't your preferred food, the point remains that God has provided a veritable feast for us. Says the Psalmist, "You cause the grass to grow for the livestock (a feast for the cows!) and plants for man to cultivate, that he may bring forth food from the earth and wine to gladden the heart of man, oil to make his face shine and bread to strengthen man's heart" (Psalm 104:14-15, ESV). Looking forward to a future day the prophet Isaiah notes that "On this mountain the LORD of hosts will make for all peoples a feast of rich food, a feast of well-aged wine, of rich food full of marrow, of aged wine well refined" (Isaiah 25:6, ESV).

God could have given humans just one food source, or made all food taste the same. Our food could have been gray sludge. Instead God gives us bread and wine, meats and marrow, fruits and vegetables, and of course, chocolate. What a good God!

Of course as we eat of this feast we do well to remember that our real hunger is for God, who can truly satisfy the longing soul, filling the hungry with good things (Psalm 107:9). We are implored to taste and see that the Lord is good (Psalm 34:8), and to know the blessing of the one who hungers and thirsts for righteousness (Matthew 5:6).

These are powerful themes of our faith, and are bound to the Christian practice of fasting, in which we deny ourselves food for a time to refocus on our hunger for God. These themes are also very much a part of our celebration of communion, where we rightly focus on Christ's sacrifice for us, but can also get in touch with our spiritual hunger, our desire to be nourished only by Him who is the bread of life.

Enjoy the feast!

DISCUSS/REFLECT

Would you say you are currently in a season of feasting or fasting in your spiritual life, filled with the fullness of God, or hungering for more of Him? What are the "spiritual foods" that God has provided to help nourish us? Are there some of these foods lacking in your spiritual diet, and if so, how could that be changed?

PRAYER

Pray together as a group in your usual manner.

Golden Cows

DISCUSS/REFLECT
What's the strangest or most expensive animal you've ever seen in person?

READ
Exodus 32:1-6

DISCUSS/REFLECT
What questions does this passage raise for you?

READ
Moses had been gone a long time. God calls for him to come up and meet on Mount Sinai. Moses went up, together with Joshua, and waited in the clouds for six days, and then on the seventh day Yahweh called to him from the cloud. "To the Israelites" we are told, "the glory of the Lord looked like a consuming fire on top of the mountain. Then Moses entered the cloud as he went on up the mountain. And he stayed on the mountain forty days and forty nights" (Exodus 24:17-18).

That the people might become restless or impatient is perhaps understandable. That they would then urge Aaron to make for them a god or gods of gold is unbelievable. God had delivered them from Pharaoh only a few months before (see Exodus 19:1), and then come to them in a spectacular display of thunder, lightening, smoke and earthquake that left the entire camp trembling (19:16f). God had then given them the

By Nicolas Poussin - Public Domain

Ten Commandments, *the very first one of which is to have no other gods before Yahweh, and the second of which is to not make an idol!* (In addition, the second commandment is one of two that gets "additional commentary" in the otherwise brief list!)

AND, after hearing all of this we learn that they again trembled in response (and begged Moses not to let God speak directly to them), following which the Lord spoke again to Moses and said, "Tell the Israelites this: 'You have seen for yourselves that I have spoken to you from heaven: Do not make any gods to be alongside me; do not make for yourselves gods of silver or gods of gold. Make an altar of earth for me and sacrifice on it your burnt offerings and fellowship offerings, your sheep and goats and your cattle. Wherever I cause my name to be honored, I will come to you and bless you" (Exodus 20:22-23).

THEN, in a ceremony of covenant commitment these same people swore to do all that the Lord had spoken, and to be obedient (Exodus 24:3-8).

What, then, could they have been thinking?! And equally astonishing, what was Aaron thinking (he had enjoyed a feast in God's very presence following the covenant ceremony – see Exodus 24:9-11)? The whole sorry episode points to the extreme and total depravity of humanity, and how quickly we turn our backs on God.

DISCUSS/REFLECT
What is your favorite mental image of God? Where does this image come from?

In what sense do we try to shape God to our image, or to familiar shapes, and what is behind that impulse? Do you see any connection between the images people have of God and a desire to somehow control God?

READ
We should note in passing the humor in this passage: when confronted by Moses for his idolatry Aaron first blamed the people ("you know how prone these people are to evil" vs 22). Then he made it sound as though the golden calf was birthed spontaneously ("they gave me the gold, and I threw it into the

fire, and out came this calf!" vs 24). This accounting of course disagrees with what we were told earlier, that Aaron took the time to make a cast in the shape of a calf with a tool (vs 4).

However it happened, we shouldn't perhaps be surprised that the final idol was a calf. Many cultures through the ages, and even today, elevate the status of cows. Generally there is a connection between cows and the life-giving milk they give, their gentle nature, their strength (that of an ox), all of which translates into cows as a strong symbol of maternal care. We noted in our first study that this was also the case in ancient Egypt: several Egyptian deities were depicted in bovine form, including Ra, who was believed to have created all forms of life.

But in the end, the calf is an idol. And as it turns out, the commandment against idolatry, in some form or another, is the most repeated of the commandments in the Bible. Idolatry is denounced more than any other sin, perhaps because God knows something about the human heart that we don't know or resist knowing: namely, that we have a strong urge to worship things other than God.

The actual commandment as it appears in Exodus 20:4 says, "You shall not make for yourself an image in the form of anything in heaven above or on the earth beneath or in the waters below. You shall not bow down to them or worship them; for I, the LORD your God, am a jealous God, punishing the children for the sin of the parents to the third and fourth generation of those who hate me, but showing love to a thousand generations of those who love me and keep my commandments."

In substance the Second Commandment is a kind of commentary and elaboration of first, that we shall have no other gods before Yahweh. Both of these commandments teach that those who worship the Judeo Christian God are called to be unapologetically exclusive in their worship, just as our God is unapologetically intolerant of other deities. There is no room for divided allegiances, and the Bible is more clear about this than perhaps anything else, from Genesis to Revelation. In the second commandment we are reminded of this exclusivity and then further told that we are to worship our God, as Jesus would later say, in spirit and in truth. God desires that our worship not be in material outward forms, and not an empty ritual, but that it be from the heart.

Beyond that, it turns out that the Second Commandment is not only the most repeated in the Bible, but it is also the second longest of the commandments, exceeded only by the commandment to remember the Sabbath. The second commandment is also the only commandment that comes with an "if/then" clause. We are told, again without apology, that God is a jealous God, in other words, and again to say, that God will tolerate no rivals for our devotion. If we honor this, all is well and good, but if we don't there will be effects that we cannot imagine, stretching out into the lives of our grandchildren and great grandchildren. This isn't some kind of mystical threat but simply a reminder that our actions have consequences that don't necessarily die when we do. For all of these reasons it is abundantly clear that God is deeply grieved when we disobey this commandment.

So how is it that the Second Commandment has relevance and meaning for our lives today? Well, let's start with what it *doesn't* forbid. Through history there have been times when people have used this commandment to form mobs, charge into cathedrals and churches, and destroy works of art depicting sacred scenes. Other less-violent interpreters have worked to keep their churches places of extreme, almost severe, austerity, lest we come to worship some part of the construction or décor of the building itself. But we know this commandment is not about austerity in the visual arts because elsewhere in Exodus God gives instructions to Moses for the building of the tabernacle, which include a curtain that is to be beautifully decorated. The ark of the covenant itself was overlaid in gold and had a cherub carved on each end.

What this commandment *does* forbid is the making of and worshipping images meant to depict God. Renowned preacher James Kennedy asks, "Have you ever looked at a picture [of yourself] and been astounded that it is absolutely the worst picture anyone has ever taken of you? If the photographer had good sense, the picture would have been torn up and never been shown to you or anybody else. But there you are, distorted and twisted. The image of you is all wrong. Your lovely self doesn't show through..." (D. James Kennedy, *Why The Ten Commandments Matter,* 47). Now think of how puny must be any image of God we would attempt... Were we to fashion an image of God and bow before it in reverence we wouldn't even be worshipping a shadow of who God really is, it would be a shadow of a shadow, which ain't much!

So how is it that we might be inclined to break this commandment? Edward Farley has written a deep analysis of the human condition in his book *Good and Evil.* One of his main points has to do with idolatry, not as the ancients practiced it with wooden or stone images, but as we practice it today. Farley's view is that idolatry is our attempt to make life secure and to remove our vulnerabilities. We do that as we satisfy ourselves with the good things of this life and then seek to guarantee those things and make them permanent. Idolatry is replacing the invisible God who creates all good things and who promises to care for us, with those good things themselves, ignoring the promises and the God behind them, or even just making God second to those promises.

DISCUSS/REFLECT

What are some things you see people around you making into idols? What kinds of things could those people do to rid themselves of those idols?

Privately reflect on your own idols and consider how you should deal with them.

READ

Revelation 4

DISCUSS/REFLECT

What questions does this passage raise for you?

READ

One sure and certain "treatment" for idolatry is to stay focused on God. The picture of the throne room of heaven we find in John's revelation is powerful and awesome. It is filled with strange wonders, including the four living creatures, "covered with eyes, in front and in back." Those eyes are a signal that we are dealing here with symbols, not literal creatures. That being said, we are shown four such creatures, the first like a lion, the second like an ox (a cow!), the third like a man, and fourth like a flying eagle (notably absent are any fish!). Commentators suggest that these four creatures are representative of the virtues such as bravery, patience, diligence, discretion, compassion, wisdom and so forth. More to the point, however, is that they are crying out day and night, 'Holy, holy, holy is the Lord God Almighty,' who was, and is, and is to come." This in turn signals twenty-four elders to fall down before the throne of God, casting down their crowns in worship, and adding their own praise (this wonderful scene of worship spills over into Revelation 5 and is worth reading as well!).

By worshipping the true God we avoid the temptation to worship that which is false. May we add our voices to the heavenly host giving praise to God, and to the Lamb who was slain, who is worth to receive power and wealth and wisdom and strength and honor and glory and praise!"

And the four living creatures said, "Amen!"

DISCUSS/REFLECT

Do you view "trust" and "faith" as synonyms? Why or why not?

What are one or two things you can do in the week ahead to better focus on worshipping the true God?

PRAYER

Pray together as a group in your usual manner.

Other books and studies by Brant Baker

The Rest of the Story, Vols 1-3

Famous Donkeys of the Bible-Six Studies for Personal or Group Study

50 Skills You Need for a Decent Chance of Success

Hands-On Christianity: Eight Studies for Small Groups

Wine in the Bible: Eight Studies for Small Groups

The Gamer Bible Study: Six Studies for Teens

The Abingdon Children's Sermon Library (3 vols) (Editor)

Let the Children Play

Teaching People to Pray

The Jesus Story (with Ben Johnson)

Welcoming The Children

Let the Children Come

Find them all on Amazon!

Made in the USA
Monee, IL
07 March 2023